I0427887

Page

ACRONYMS

ASEAN	Association of Southeast Asian Nations
ASG	Abu-Sayyaf Group (Al Harakatol Al Islamiyah)
EEZ	Exclusive Economic Zone
GWOT	Global War on Terrorism. The military campaign undertaken by the United States since the attacks of 9/11/2001.
KALAHI	*Kapit-Bisig Laban sa Kahirapan* (Linking Arms Against Poverty)
MDT	Mutual Defence Treaty
MILF	Moro Islamic Liberaton Front
MNLF	Moro National Liberation Front
NSP	National Security Policy
NSS	National Security Strategy
NPA	New People's Army (Bagong Hukbong Bayan)

ILLUSTRATIONS

CHAPTER 1

INTRODUCTION

Background

Security is only one dimension of a pattern of international relations that make the
Southeast Asian subsystem an important unit of the global international system.
— Donald E. Weatherbee, *International Relations in Southeast Asia:*
The Struggle for Autonomy

The determination of any one nation to act unilaterally in order to combat

terrorism represents a significant development within the international community and

may result in second and third-order effects to the international community. The desire to

act unilaterally in the exercise of state sovereignty, may sometimes conflict with the

strategic goals of other states, thus resulting in further tension, which may devolve into

conflict between states or coaltions. State leaders and others in positions of power may

identify and bring attention to threats to the status quo via the securitization process.[1]

This process may then illegitimize the unilateral actions of states because they may fail to

address threats recognized by regional or international partners. Therefore, few states opt

to act unilaterally rather than with partners. Instead, states opt to align and form coaltions

in order to gain legitimacy of effort in the eyes of the international community, such as

the quickly formed coalition of the willing created to conduct Operation Stabilise in East

Timor in 1999.[2]

---

[1]T. O'Connor, "The Concept of Securitization," *MegaLinks in Criminal Justice*,
March 9, 2011, http://www.drtomoconnor.com/2010/2010lect01a.htm. (November 1,
2011).

[2]Alan Ryan, "The Strong Lead-Nation Model in an ad hoc Coalition of the
Willing: Operation Stabilise in East Timor," *International Peacekeeping* 9, no. 1 (Spring

Within these attempts to form coalitions and act in concert with other states, opportunity exists to both solve the immediate problem of the security issue, as well as simultaneously advancing strategic agendas in order to preclude situations where unilateral action is required. In other words, states can gain economy of scale during efforts to ally with other nations to solve common security issues by aligning goals which are more strategic in nature at the same time and advance strategic goals.

The U.S. has taken advantage of such opportunities during the past ten years. Since the inception of the current Global War on Terror (GWOT), the U.S. has attempted to avoid a myopic view of the possible threats which exist in the current operating environment.[3] Specifically, the U.S. sought early-on the cooperation of the Republic of the Philippines (RP), a long-standing ally of the U.S.[4] The U.S. sought out this cooperation in order to preclude the development of another front in the GWOT, due to the perception by the U.S. that certain elements of radical Islamic groups in the Southeast Asian region, including the RP, may escalate their activities in the region.

This partnership with the Republic of the Philippines was illuminated specifically in the *2002 National Security Strategy* by President George W. Bush and confirmed that the U.S. viewed the "deepened cooperation on counter-terrorism with our alliance

---

2002): 23-34. This was an international peace-keeping operation in East Timor in 1999, in which the U.S. military supported a coalition force led by Australia and New Zealand.

[3]Although the GWOT acronym is no longer used to refer to efforts to combat terrorism, it is used in this paper due to the fact that some of the documents referenced contain the acronym and it reduced the possibility of confusion during the research process by providing continuity of terminology.

[4]Washington File, http://usinfo.org/wf-archive/2001/011120/epf214.htm. (accessed August 21, 2011).

partners in Thailand and the Philippines"[5] as a step towards advancing national strategy

interests. Thus, this aligned the pursuit of strategic goals between the U.S. and the

Republic of the Philippines with the alliance formed in order to combat the terrorist threat

in Southeast Asia posed by groups such as the Abu Sayyaf Group (ASG), the Moro

Islamic Liberation Front (MILF), and others.

The Republic of the Phlippines also viewed the alliance with the U.S. as a means

to advance strategic goals while meeting immediate security needs. In her 2002 State of

the Nation Address, then-President of the Philippines Gloria Macapagal-Arroyo noted

that "[the Philippines has] gained powerful allies in our domestic war against terrorism. I

am certain that our increased international visibility will continue generating capital

inflows for the Philippines."[6] In other words, while President Arroyo clearly identified

the importance of aligning with the U.S. in efforts to combat an internal security threat,

she also noted that these efforts would result in an ancillary effect of advancing the

overall strategic goals of the RP. By aligning with the U.S. the RP could advance their

internal goals of economic prosperity and security.

Certainly, many nations recognize the value of establishing coalition-type

structures in order to bolster legitimacy and effectiveness through unity of effort in

attaining strategic goals. For example, the U.S. specifically mentions that "effective

---

[5]President of the United States, *National Security Strategy*, September 2002.
http://merln.ndu.edu/whitepapers/USnss2002.pdf (accessed October 11, 2011).

[6]Gloria Macapagal-Arroyo, "Second State of the Nation Address," July 22, 2002,
http://www.gov.ph/2002/07/22/gloria-macapagal-arroyo-second-state-of-the-nation-
address-july-22-2002/ (accessed October 11, 2011).

action often turns on the political will of coalitions of countries"[7] within the current *National Security Strategy*. It becomes advantageous for states to leverage alliances and partnerships in order to achieve these objectives while maintaining their sovereignty and international standing.

One factor which provides a catalyst for strengthening coalitions and partnerships involves shared strategy. Certainly, it is a given that all states have self-interest in mind where strategic goals are concerned. However, while strategic goals may be self-centered, they need not be mutually exclusive. For example, in his July 25, 2011 State of the Nation Address, Philippine President Benigno S. Aquino, III asserted that "[w]e do not wish to increase tensions with anyone, but we must let the world know that we are ready to protect what is ours."[8] While such sentiment may appear at first blush to represent an aggressive, nationalist, protectionist stance, the fact is that the RP works tirelessly to partner with other nations in order to advance strategic goals and leverage partnerships in a positive way.[9]

The fundamental premise of this paper is that areas of shared streategic interest exist between the U.S. and the RP, specifically regarding the Southeast Asian region wherein the RP is located. Further, that identification and exploitation these shared

---

[7]President of the United States, *National Security Strategy,* May 2010, http://www.whitehouse.gov/sites/default/files/rss_viewer/national_security_strategy.pdf (accessed October 11, 2011).

[8]Benigno S. Aquino III (July 25, 2011). Second State of the Nation Address (English Translation), http://www.gov.ph/2011/07/25/benigno-s-aquino-iii-second-state-of-the-nation-address-july-25-2011-en/ (accessed October 15, 2011).

[9]National Security Council Group, *National Security Policy: Securing the Gains of Democracy,* 2011, 5.

strategic interests may bear fruit in advancing the strategic interests of both nations quicker, more effectively, more efficiently, and more legitimately, than either nation may realize alone.

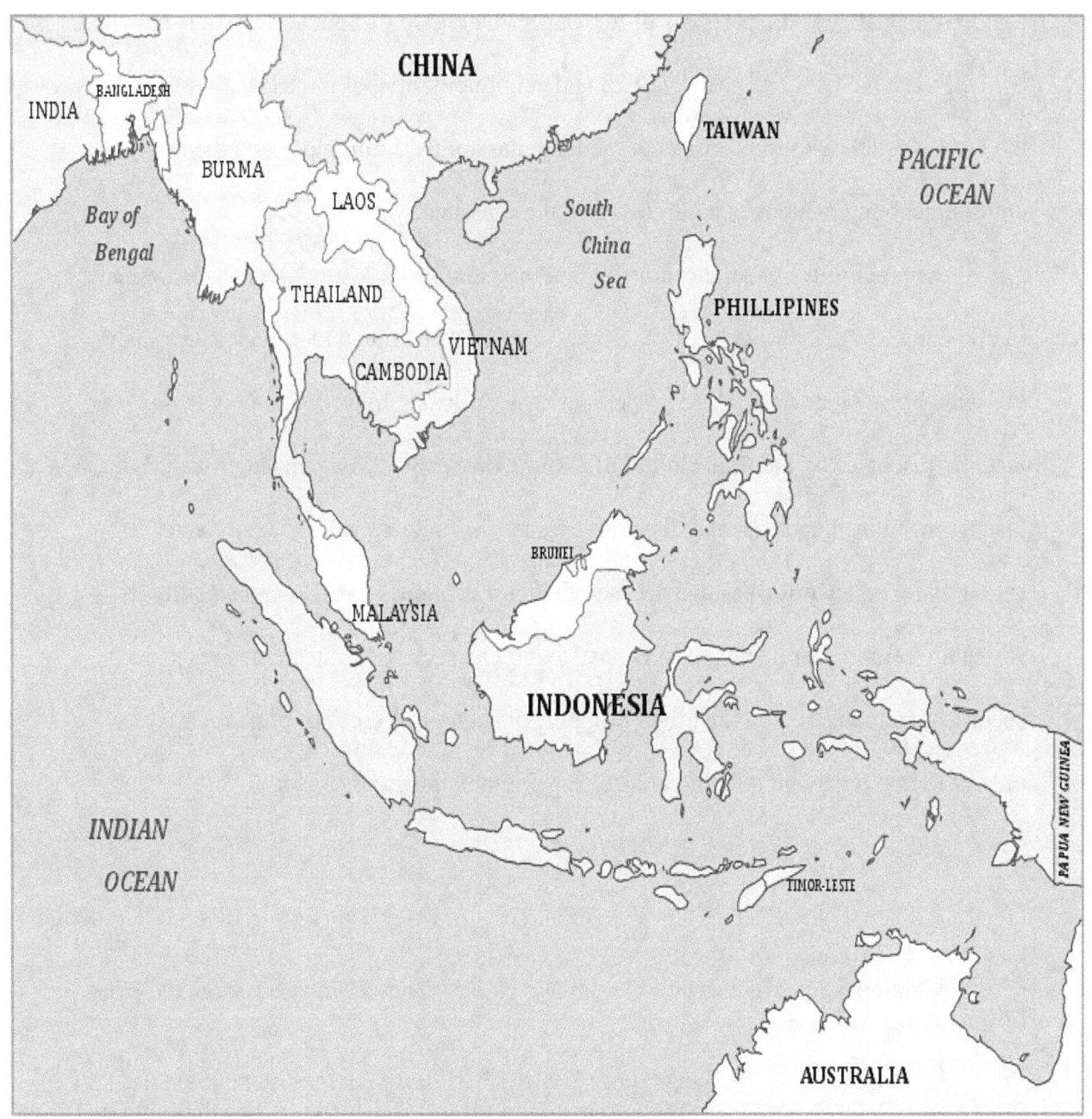

Figure 1.   Map of Southeast Asia

Source: ....

Primary Research Question

The primary question this paper attempts to address is whether strategic points of convergence exist between U.S. and the RP pertaining to combating terrorism within the region of the RP. For the purposes of this paper, the region of Southeast Asia is bounded by the Exclusive Economic Zone (EEZ) and contiguous zone of the RP.[10] In other words, the area of Southeast Asia consists of the land mass of the Philippines and the littoral environment out to 200 nautical miles from the coastline.

As previously stated, the strategic interests and goals of any given state are, most likely, unique to that particular state. However, it may be argued that most states share the same broad strategic goals (e.g., prosperity, security).[11] Indeed, this very theme was recently discussed by Dr. Paul Collier of Oxford University, who penned an article discussing "three important and distinctive issues for building state capacity and encouraging policy priorities that are beneficial for economic growth and stability"[12] which are certainly strategic goals. By narrowing the focus of strategic desires to a specific geographic region (i.e., the Philippines) and topical area (i.e., terrorism), it is presumed that it may be possible to discover similar strategic interests.

---

[10]National Security Council Group, *National Security Policy: Securing the Gains of Democracy*, 2011, 30.

[11]John T. Kuehn, "Talking Grand Strategy," *Military Review* 90, no. 5 (September-October 2011): 76. Military historian John T. Kuehn addresses these internal, national goals in his recent article on the importance of grand strategy.

[12]Paul Collier, "State Building: Job Creation, Investment Promotion, and the Provision of Basic Services," *PRISM* 2, no. 4 (September 2011): 17-30.

Secondary Research Questions

Secondary research questions that emerge from the primary question necessarily address the policy implementation options available for the U.S. and the RP to combat terrorist threats in Southeast Asia. For example, a secondary research question that the researcher intends to investigate is whether the U.S. and the RP have adopted patterns of strategies over time to contend with security issues.

Additionally, what policy initiatives have emerged from these security strategies and how would the RP implement them? If one investigates these issues, it would become possible to recommend potential strategic initiatives and programs which could address real-world issues, rather than merely hypothetical situations and abstract possibilities.

Whereas the primary research question reflects the focused and narrow nature of the study, the secondary research questions anticipated by the researcher further refine the study towards specific strategic goals and policy implementation options which both nations may synthesize in order to gain more economical results.

Significance

Pursuing strategic goals and objectives is vital to the success of any nation. The emphasis on strategy is so great that many nations include constitutional mandates which require the head of state to address the national audience periodically. During these addresses, the head of state assures the audience that goals are being pursued, as well as updating them on the status. Studies that attempt to identify more effective and efficient ways to pursue strategic goals are a fruitful avenue for academic endeavor.

Specifically, this study is significant due to the relationship shared by the U.S. and the RP. The RP has been an important strategic concern for the U.S. since the 19th century. In the modern era, presidents of the U.S. have expressed concern about the stability of the region for decades. In 1985, for example, then-President Ronald Reagan noted that "[w]e have a serious problem with the Philippines–a communist takeover is a distinct possibility."[13]

While the researcher anticipates that this study will augment the existing body of knowledge regarding strategic thought, the researcher also realizes that a more significant contribution to the body of knowledge would require an intensive and in-depth study beyond the scale and scope of this paper, requiring a significant investement in time and money to complete. This paper may contribute to illuminating shared strategy study and the recommendations for future research may identify a realistic options in this field.

<u>Assumptions</u>

The first assumption presumes that an interest exists within the U.S. to identify areas where strategic goals may be aligned with other states, specifically the RP. This presumption also assumes that the cooperative and complementary nature of the relationship between the U.S. and the RP will continue for the foreseeable future due to the stated "enduring interest of the [Philippines] to forge harmonious engagement and relationship with other nations."[14] Additionally, an alignment of strategic interests, if

---

[13]Ronald Reagan, *The Reagan Diaries*, ed. Douglas Brinkley (New York: Harper Collins Publishers, 2007), 351.

[14]Republic of the Philippines, *2011-2016 National Security Policy: Securing the Gains of Democracy* (Manila: Bureau of Printing, 2011), 5.

pursued, should result in a more efficient and economical advancement of these interests. The last assumption is that shared strategic areas of interest exist between the U.S. and the RP that could be identified that pertain specifically to the geographic region identified (i.e. Southeast Asia).

Scope

This paper provides background information regarding the current GWOT and terrorist activity within the RP in order to contextualize the reason why the researcher is interested in investigating the possibility of aligned strategic interests. In short, national security strategy is a persistent issue that demands current attention. During the current, protracted involvement of the U.S. in efforts to eradicate terrorism in Southwest Asia, the issue has gained momentum and garnered even more attention.

In order to demonstrate the volume of interest which exists pertaining to the national security strategy of the U.S., the researcher performed an impromptu search on the Internet using the "Google Scholar" search engine for the terms "u.s. national security strategy." The search resulted in approximately 2,300,000 results for the search terms. While the researcher certainly did not attempt to investigate all of these sources, it became quite evident early on that national security strategy represented a viable research topic for continued exploration. Unfortunately, with the body of knowledge being this large already, it became unclear whether the researcher would be able to add to the body of knowledge on the topic in any meaningful way.

The scope of this paper encompasses the concept that strategic alignment between the U.S. and the RP exists. Specifically, the issue of terrorism was employed as a means of contextualizing why the issue of national security strategy demands attention and, additionally, why the researcher believes that performing a comparative analysis of the national security strategies of two nations may be a viable research topic. It is not meant to provide a specific limitation to the scope of the study, nor to develop a particular theme for the research, or to "drive" the research efforts. To do so would remove this study from the strategic realm and, instead, transfer the project to the operational realm.

Limitations

The researcher confronted a limitation based on the available resources for information concerning the proposed topic. The researcher attempted to contact esperts within the RP, including military officials with strategic positions within the Armed Forces of the Philippines in order to gain valuable insight into the strategic interests of the RP. The researcher received few replies from these attempts, none of which were actual iterations of policy, but merely guidance on where to locate information. The researcher was not attempting to contact these individuals in order to conduct interviews via electronic media or telephone, or other correspondence. The researcher contacted these sources only in an attempt to obtain more detailed documentary evidence and to, perhaps, locate a better source for policy documents and other research sources.

Lastly, the research was limited to unclassified sources in order to facilitate access to a broader range of documentation and strategic literature. This limitation was also required because of the fact that the researcher would not be able to access parallel classified resources from the RP in order to compare them with sources from the U.S.

Delimitations

The researcher delimited the study in order to narrow the scope of the project enough to mitigate the time constraint by reviewing literature from within the past ten years that pertained to the subject matter. This delimitation allows the researcher to review subject matter of sufficient quantity to gain breadth and depth of understanding of the material. Additionally, by reviewing only the more recent literature and documentation, the researcher was able to develop conclusions and recommendations based on the more contemporary body of knowledge and thought. This includes the relevant documents and public statements (e.g., State of the Nation Speeches and doctrine material) as well as the published literature pertaining to the subject matter.

Summary

The RP is the only predominantly Christian nation in Southeast Asia. The country has enjoyed a long and mutually-beneficial relationship with the U.S. since the RP became a possession of the U.S. as a result of the 1898 Treaty of Paris. Although Christian, the nation faces continuing pressure and internal friction from Muslim separatist groups, owing to its initial contact with Arab traders during the period between the 8th and 13th centuries. Virtually since the birth of the nation, there has been animosity between the Muslim south and the Christian north. These internal problems provide the genesis for the need to examine strategies to combat terrorism in the region and how the RP may exploit gains in combating terrorism by aligning strategies with other nations, such as the U.S.

This chapter presented an introduction to the study, including the purpose and background. Chapter 2 will present a review of the literature relevant to the topic, including official documents and policies, as well as official addresses and speeches.

CHAPTER 2

LITERATURE REVIEW

The purpose of the literature review is to examine the current body of knowledge regarding the strategic posture of the RP pertaining to independent security. In other words, the literature review identifies specific policy and literature establishing how the RP would cooperate with other nations (i.e., the U.S.) in efforts to combat, eradicate, deter, or prevent military or non-state actor insurgencies in order to meet their strategic security goals.

The literature review was structured topically, progressing from the more broad issues to the more specific. Incorporated throughout this topical arrangement, additionally, the perspectives of the U.S. and the Republic of the Philippines were interspersed in order to attempt to point out similarities or differences pertaining to each topic.

Grand Strategy

In order to engage in a discussion and analysis of strategic goals, one must first gain an understanding of the overall meaning and importance of strategy. To carry this further, in order to ascertain the strategic goals of a nation, one must comprehend the different levels at which strategy may be developed.

Recently, military historian John T. Kuehn addresses the debate as to whether or not the U.S. possesses a grand strategy. Specifically, Kuehn asserts that "[a] good place to start looking for a coherent grand strategy is in the Constitution of the United States, from which we can extrapolate a coherent grand strategy,"[15] and continues on to identify the mandates outlined in the Preamble to the Constitution as the grand strategy of the U.S.

While this approach may be satisfactory for states with enduring constitutions, it must be amended somewhat in states that have adopted multiple constitutions. For example, the current Constitution of the Republic of the Philippines was adopted in 1987, after a provisional constitution was adopted in 1986, following the People Power Revolution that removed Ferdinand Marcos from office. While these two iterations of the Constitution of the Philippines are quite similar, other Constitutions of the Philippines provide a a stark philosophical contrast.

For example, there is a distinct shift in focus between the 1935 and 1943 Constitutions of the Philippines, with the preambles specifically mentioning the anticipated independence of the nation. Therefore, the application of Kuehn's assertion is more suited to states with enduring constitutional frameworks. Application of this type of strategic analysis of constitutional priorities to states with more fluid or dynamic governments proves a bit more challenging, as the moods and personalities of the nation shift.

Arthur Lykke, in his discussion of the ends, ways, and means model to analyze military strategy, touches on grand strategy as a means of identifying the distinction between the over-arching nature of grand strategy and the more specific focus of military strategy. Lykke advances the published Joint Chiefs of Staff (JCS) definition of grand strategy (in 1985) as "The art and science of developing and using the political,

---

[15]Kuehn, "Talking Grand Strategy," 76.

14

economic, and psychological powers of a nation, together with its armed forces, during peace and war, to secure national objectives."[16]

Lykke asserts that grand strategy encompasses military strategy, while including other components of the state's strategic agenda within its purview. He also counters the argument that military components are merely supportive of national strategies, not components of the national strategy. Lykke points out that military decisions made in the absence of conflict shape the environment in efforts to deter future conflict. Therefore, they are integral parts of the strategic decision-making considerations.

Lykke moves on to discuss his model of how the military strategy supports national security, depicted as a stool.[17] One may easily extrapolate this model to the level of grand strategy, with national security acting as one of the legs of the stool which supports grand strategy. Simply put, much as Lykke's model depicts objectives, concepts, and resources supporting military strategy and national security; one may envision military, political, economic, and other strategies supporting the stable platform of national security, upon which, grand strategy rests.

Daniel Drezner, somewhat in contrast to Lykke and Kuehn, posits that there is less of a requirement for a formalized grand strategy than one may think. Instead, Drezner contends that the actions of a state are far more important and influential than

---

[16]Chairman, Joint Chiefs of Staff. Joint Publication (JP) 1, *Dictionary of Military and Associated Terms* (Washington, DC: Government Printing Office, 1985), 244.

[17]Arthur F. Lykke, Jr., "Toward and Understanding of Military Strategy," in *Military Strategy: Theory and Application* (Carlisle Barracks, PA: Government Printing Office, 1989), 182.

their stated policy objectives.[18] This may be a blinding flash of the obvious, but is worth capturing as an important concept to retain. However, Drezner's perspective of what constitutes grand strategy differs from the perspectives of Kuehn and Lykke in an important, yet subtle way.

Drezner unveils this difference in perspectives through a reference to the grand strategies advanced by the current President of the United States. While this may not seem to indicate a difference in perspectives, upon further examination an important point emerges. By asserting that the current, sitting President has advanced two separate and distinct grand strategies in less than one full term in office, Drezner clearly indicates that he believes grand strategies are more fluid than either Kuehn and Lykke anticipate. Significantly, this perception also lends to the erosion of the importance of grand strategies and begins to draw them into a lower level of strategic thought.

Additionally, Drezner appears to isolate grand strategy to the realm of political and international relations, rather than incorporating all facets of national strategy into the development of a grand strategy. Admittedly, this may be an unfair interpretation, since Drezner may simply have been attempting to conserve space in his essay. However, discussion of grand strategy, if one adopts the perspectives of Kuehn and Lykke over that of Drezner, would necessarily require an in-depth analysis of multiple facets of the national policy initiatives, rather than a mere passing mention or allusion to them, as Drezner makes.

---

[18]Daniel W. Drezner, "Does Obama have a Grand Strategy?," *Foreign Affairs* 90, no. 4 (July-August 2011): 61.

Indeed, when Drezner continues to expound upon the meaning of grand strategy, one becomes aware of a narrowing of focus. Drezner seems to be content to speak about the development of grand strategy as it pertains to foreign policy alone. Further, he speaks of grand strategy separately, not as an encompassing tool of national policy which factors in economic strategy, political strategy, social strategy and others, but rather as a unique entity which parallels other strategic initiatives, while maintaining its respective distance.

In *Grand Strategies in War and Peace*, Paul Kennedy compiles the works of several scholars contending with the issues of how grand strategies impact various states of conflict and peace. While this volume contained numerous thoughts and theories, Kennedy illuminates the importance of applying strategic considerations to periods of national conflict and non-conflict. He states that "a true grand strategy was now concerned with peace as much as (perhaps even more than) with war,"[19] confirming Sir B. H. Liddell Hart's maxim that planning for peace is as important as planning for conflict.

Kennedy's book is relevant to the research due to the fact that, as Kennedy himself points out that "[t]he crux of grand strategy lies therefore in policy . . . the capacity of the nation's leaders to bring together all of the elements . . . for the preservation and enhancement of the nation's long-term . . . best interests."[20] Certainly, then, if one identifies common interests (e.g., national security), one may also identify

---

[19]Paul Kennedy, *Grand Strategy in War and Peace: Toward a Broader Definition* (New Haven, CT: Yale University Press, 1992), 4.

[20]Ibid., 5.

strategic initiatives which are common between nations. In fact, the existence of this possibility is the genesis for the research project.

Security Strategy

Narrowing the focus of the research from grand strategy to security strategy results in more relevant literature becoming available. Additionally, definitions and paradigms which describe and address specific issues of security strategy become much less ambiguous. There appears to be much less disagreement between the nature of security strategy than exists regarding the nature of grand strategy.

An abundance of literature exists pertaining to the inter-related security strategies of the U.S. and the RP. As previously noted, the RP was awarded as a possession of the U.S. at the conclusion of the Spanish-American War, and this probably accounts for the amount of literature regarding the shared security interests of the two nations. Since that time, the U.S. and the RP have been (arguably) inextricably linked to each other, with the U.S. establishing and maintaining bases in the country until 1993. Although some of this literature is dated, there is also contemporary literature regarding shared security strategies of the two nations due to the current terrorist threats which exist within the RP. Of note, the continuity of thought regarding the importance of security in the RP to the U.S. lends to the contention that the security of the RP has been (and continues to be) a national interest of the U.S.

Claude A. Buss discusses the evolution of various strategic security cooperative measures that have existed between the U.S. and the RP. Notably, he discusses the 1951 Mutual Defense Treaty (MDT) that was enacted between the U.S. and the RP. This treaty provided a level of security against potential threats in the region for both nations. Buss points out that the treaty, in effect, acknowledged that an attack on either party to the treaty would pose a threat to the overall security of both nations.[21]

Buss continues to explore the concerns that previous American administrations have faced regarding the boundaries of the 1951 MDT. These concerns have become more relevant today than they were at the time of Buss's examination of them, with the advent of modern insurgencies and counterinsurgency activity by the U.S. Specifically, it becomes a contemporary issue of note that the U.S. must examine the 1951 MDT and determine whether it includes intervention on behalf of the RP by the U.S. in order to quell the ongoing insurgencies in the RP.

The creation, maintenance, and sustainment of alliances is a key component of the security strategy of the RP. Renato Cruz De Castro notes that the nation has worked diligently to improve relations with the U.S. in efforts to contend with insurgencies and terrorist threats to the RP.[22] Leveraging the alliance with the U.S. must be conducted while bearing in mind that there are other world powers that may aid the RP in achieving its strategic goals. For example, the U.S. has played a huge role in providing external security for the RP since 1946.[23] Included in this role, as De Castro notes, is the comprehensive funding of the Armed Forces of the Philippines (AFP) during their Capability Upgrade Program that is intended to significantly improve the ability of the

---

[21]Claude A. Buss, *The United States and the Philippines: Background for Policy* (Washington, DC: American Enterprise Institute for Public Policy Research, 1977), 113.

[22]Renato Cruz De Castro, "Engaging Both the Eagle and the Dragos: The Philippines' Precarious and Futile Attempt in Equi-Balancing," *Pacific Focus* 25, no. 3 (December 2010): 357.

[23]Ibid., 359.

Philippine government to provide for its own security, both internally and externally.[24] In short, the U.S. and the RP have revitalized a key security strategy for the Southeast Asian region recently through cooperative initiatives designed to enhance the ability of the Philippines to play a role in regional security against, mainly, terrorist threats. There are, however, limits to just far these cooperative efforts may go.

The current Constitution of the Philippines, ratified in 1987, explicity prohibits permanent basing of foreign military forces within the country and, in effect, precludes foreign military forces from engaging in prolonged military operations within the borders of the country.[25] However, it does not specifically address the provisions of the 1951 MDT[26]. Therefore, does the MDT satisfy the 1987 constitution's requirement that permanent presence of foreign troops in the country be negotiated formally, since the current Constitution of the Philippines did not formally void the MDT? If so, is the U.S. acting in accordance with the MDT by assisting in counterinsurgency efforts in the Philippines?

Buss concluded his study in 1977, so it cannot effectively address these questions due to the fact that the RP was operating under a completely different constitution at the time. Though the constitutions have changed, there were threats similar to those that exist today within the RP. The New People's Army (NPA) is an outgrowth of the Huk rebels,

---

[24]Ibid., 361.

[25]These provisions may be formally circumvented via a negotiated treaty between the Congress of the Philippines and any other nation. Current U.S. forces operate in an advisory capacity in training exercises with the AFP.

[26]Nor should a Constitution be expected to address every specific treaty in effect. The author is merely pointing out that the current Constitution and the 1951 MDT appear to have areas of direct conflict that should be investigated and, if needed, resolved.

who made their military debut during the Japanese occupation of the RP in World War II. This group was extremely active in the northern RP during the period when Buss wrote his report. Admittedly, the GWOT was not in existence and nations viewed these types of insurgencies differently than they do now.

In his article, "The Philippine Bases and U.S. Pacific Strategy," Gregory P. Corning begins to merge the strategies of the U.S. and the RP. At the time Corning wrote the article, the U.S. still maintained Clark Air Base and the Subic Bay Naval Station and the RP was still viewed as a key component of the Pacific presence of the U.S. The insights into the strategic points of convergence which Corning points out support the contention that there may be similarities or complimentary objectives in strategy.

As Corning notes "[a]n important aspect of peacetime strategy is security assistance programs which work to strengthen relationships and improve the interoperability of forces."[27] Corning's article itself concerns a slightly more specific aspect of strategy (i.e., Pacific strategy) than that of grand strategy. His assertion that partnerships and assistance programs are vital to pursuing successful security strategies parallels statements in both the current National Security Strategies of the U.S. and the RP.

Donald Weatherbee addresses security strategies in his book, *International Relations in Southeast Asia: The Struggle for Autonomy*. Weatherbee addresses the issues mainly from the perspective of the RP, since his text attempts to discuss which stimuli affect the political environment in Southeast Asia and how the various states in the region

---

[27]Gregory P. Corning, "The Philippine Bases in U. S. Pacific Strategy," *Pacific Affairs* 63, no. 1 (Spring 1990): 8.

inter-relate to influence the environment and either encourage or discourage outside actors from engaging in the region. He makes notable arguments which support the suggestion that there are mutually supported strategic interests and goals between the U.S. and the RP.

Referring to then-President Gloria Arroyo, Weatherbee notes, "that fundamental to the Philippines' security is its strategic relationship to the U.S."[28] Some may presume that this strategic relationship focuses on the struggles the RP has encountered in dealing with insurgencies within its southern regions (e.g., MNLF, MILF, ASG). However, as Weatherbee notes, the Philippines has struggled with non-state actors within its borders, such as the NPA, as well as external threats to its security from state actors such as China.[29]

Weatherbee's text encompasses the entire Southeast Asian region, not limiting itself to merely discussing the RP. Weatherbee not only notes the existence of a strategic relationship between the RP and the U.S., but also points out that leaders within the RP recognize this relationship and that these leaders consciously make policy decisions based upon this relationship. It may be presumed that this is not a unilateral effort, but rather, an effort supported by and coordinated with the U.S.

<u>Strategic Thought</u>

Additionally, academic literature pertaining to the cultural development of strategic thought was reviewed. Nicola Baker and Leonard C. Sebastian examine the

---

[28]Weatherbee, *International Relations in Southeast Asia,* 37.

[29]Ibid., 36.

peculiarities of strategic policy development within Asia and compare this with the development of strategy in European nations. In this article, the authors explain their theory that dangers lie ahead for those who believe that security strategies from Europe and Western nations can serve as templates for similar needs in Asia. These dangers arise from cultural variances on the origins of strategic thought which exist between Western European cultures and the cultures of Asian nations.

Baker and Sebastian point out that European states shared their desire for a balance of power in order to resist external security threats. Additionally, their similar cultural heritage and religious backgrounds fostered the genesis of this strategic culture.[30] Conversely, Asian states arose out of a variety of cultural and philosophical paradigms, resulting in a need for state security. Internal friction and threats, compounded with external antagonism, provided the genesis of the need for state security.[31]

Baker and Sebastian's article proved helpful in analyzing the possible reasons that U.S. strategy and the strategy of the RP may focus on the same priorities, yet for varying reasons. In other words, while the goals may be the same, the perception for the need to achieve that particular goal may be different. Additionally, the variance in perspectives of security strategy may result in differences in implementation, differences in prioritization, and differences in evaluation of success. This would require any interaction between these two states to factor in a possible need to align agendas in addition to aligning strategic interests.

---

[30]Nicola Baker and Leonard C. Sebastian, "The Problem with Parachuting: Strategic Studies and Security in the Asia/Pacific Region," *Strategic Studies and Security* 18, no. 3 (1995): 16.

[31]Ibid., 19.

For example, while the RP and the U.S. may both desire security for the littorals around Cebu as a strategic priority for inter-island commerce and transit, one party may expect a more aggressive pursuit of this security goal and become concerned when the other party appears to be less aggressive with achieving this goal. Therefore, it becomes imperative that any discussion of mutual strategic goals accounts for the possible misinterpretation of the way in which these strategies are implemented in order to ensure unity of effort and realization of these goals. Simply, such cultural issues compound the already complicated prospect of developing supportive security strategies.

Constructing and implementing security organizations is a complex undertaking in and of itself, as Acharya noted in his article about Southeast Asian regional security communities.[32] Acharya also points out that it becomes "useful to have a narrower and somewhat different set of indicators for identifying the conditions for a security community outside of the specific socio-political setting of the North Atlantic area,"[33] thus synthesizing the premises of cultural complexity with the intricate nature of formulating security co-ops.

The desire to align mutually-supportive and beneficial policy initiatives arguably bears more weight than the variances in cultural perception of strategic goals and objectives. This area is also touched upon by Acharya, who notes that the successful integration of supportive policies in areas of other strategic interest (e.g., trade) exponentially increase the desire to implement supportive policy initiatives in more

---

[32]Amitav Acharya, "A Regional Security Community in Southeast Asia?" *Strategic Studies and Security* 18, no. 3 (1995): 175.

[33]Ibid., 177.

24

important policy areas. This assertion gains some validity when one explores the relationship between the U.S. and the RP. The historical relationship between the two nations has grown through various initiatives, and has resulted in the two nations entering into the 1951 MDT, codifying the relationship and desire to pursue shared objectives.

Policy Statements

The literature review includes an addendum that contains a review of recent policy statements. This review was conducted in order to gain a more comprehensive understanding of the strategic perspectives under which the U.S. and the RP operate. These policy statements included addresses by the heads of state, and discuss various strategic initiatives and programs in a broad sense and provide the genesis for the implementation of strategic programs within a nation. The review also serves as a ready reference for the analysis.

Republic of the Philippines

On October 21, 2010, President of the Republic of the Philippines, Benigno S. Aquino, III, signed a memorandum which required National Security Advisor/National Security Council Director-General, to develop a national security strategy for 2010-2016.[34] The RP released the final product in 2011 as a national directive that outlines the national security policy for the RP for the years 2011-2016.

This memorandum intended the national security policy to capitalize on the provisions of the *Human Security Act of 2007*. The Third Special Session of the

---

[34]Memorandum Order No. 6 by the President of the Philippines, October 21, 2010, http://www.gov.ph/2010/10/21/memorandum-order-no-6/ (accessed October 11, 2011).

Thirteenth Congress of the Republic of the Philippines passed this act in order to codify the definitions of terrorism and other activities subversive and destructive to the government of the RP. The intent was to facilitate the development of policy initiatives that could brind the instruments of national pwer to bear in combating terrorism and ensuring national security.

The memorandum itself is fairly insignificant in importance to the comparison of security strategy between the U.S. and the Philippines. However, the resultant *2011-2016 National Security Policy* (*NSP*) asserts the foundational beliefs of the Philippine nation. The *NSP* also confirms the dedication of the nation to the stability of the international environment. Philosophically, the RP views its obligations as layered, with their focus widening from the inherent obligation of the national government to the people, towards a world-wide commitment to the stability of the environment. To overview the *NSP*, it focuses internally and externally on security issues for the RP. By taking this bifurcated view of the operating environment, the *NSP* develops a holistic approach to securing the nation because all possible factors that may affect the nation are considered.

Foremost, the *NSP* recognizes that the government itself must be secure. The *NSP* argues that a detailed social contract, established by the current President, can best achieve this security.[35] Historically, the RP has undergone several revolutionary changes in government. Additionallyk, several armed insurgencies currently threaten the nation. Therefore, there must be an explicit, easily understood communication of the relationship between the government and the constituency.

---

[35]Republic of the Philippines, *2011-2016 National Security Policy*, 5.

Notably, the RP includes the alignment of efforts to combat terrorism with other nations in the *NSP*.[36] The *NSP* contains the themes of external partnership and cooperation throughout and emphasizes the fact that, as a developing nation with limited power projection capability, it must focus its efforts for securitn the environment inward. External focal points require the assistance of other, more developed and capable states. The premise of this paper advances the argument that even developed nations must engage in cooperative efforts in order to maximize security. Parternships and alliances become exponentially more important as developing nations struggle to achieve stability and security.

The United States

In order to conduct an effective comparative analysis of the national security strategies of the two nations, the research included a review of the *National Security Strategy (NSS) of the United States of America*. The four overarching interests espoused by the *2010 NSS* include: security, prosperity, values and international order,[37] and represent the U.S.' overall strategic methodolgy towards achieving the desired level of national security. The *NSS* of the U.S. articulates, to a more specific degree, the goals of the grand strategy of the U.S., as found in the Constitution.

Previous discussion included the importance of constitutional mandates, as well as their bearing on the interpretation and identification of a nation's grand strategy. In the case of the U.S. Constitution, although the Constitution is malleable in the sense that it is

---

[36]Ibid., 9.

[37]The President of the United States, *2010 National Security Strategy* (Washington, DC: Government Printing Office, 2010), Table of Contents.

subject to amendment and provides mechanisms for change, it has remained strategically consistent in spirit since its inception. By this, it is meant that the constitutional mandate to the government to provide for the security of the nation contributes to the grand strategy of the nation. The maintenance of the national security provides one of the "foremost reasons for government to exist."[38] Therefore, the facet of grand strategy that contends with the nation's security exists within the framework of the U. S. Constitution.

If one accepts the premise that the U. S. Constitution establishes the grand strategy of the nation, including the mandate for the government to provide for the national security, then how does the nation manage the changes in the environment in order to provide a secure community for the U.S. to operate in? The *NSS* refines these grand strategic objectives into a more manageable and attainable strategy for the security of the nation. In short, grand strategy (as noted previously) is the highest level of strategic thought, and security strategy is a component of that grand strategy, focusing the instruments of national power upon the objective of national security.

The *NSS* does not merely focus military means on the objectives of national security. Rather, as noted, the *NSS* incorporates and synthesizes the entirety of the instruments of national power upon the national security objectives of the U.S. The *NSS* creates a synergy between the instruments of national power, linking these instruments towards each of the four specified interests. Notably, and pertinent to the subject of this paper, one of the stated objectives of the national security policy is to build and foster alliances with other nations in order to stabilize international order. Therefore, because

---

[38]Findlaw, "Maintenance of National Security and the First Amendment," http://caselaw.lp.findlaw.com/data/constitution/amendment01/13.html (accessed March 11, 2012).

alliances with other nations are an objective of the *NSS*, examinations are required of the goals, policies, and strategies of other nations. These examinations and studies of the strategies of other nations aid in determining the best ways to meet the strategic interests of the U.S. through cooperative efforts. Just as one must study an enemy, one must also study friends and potential friends.

The Asia-Pacific region represents an area of concern within the strategic environment. Indeed, this region is specifically mentioned repeatedly within the *NSS* and other documents, and is noted as an area deserving more focus in the future.[39] The RP is recognized as a continuing ally for the pursuit of strategic security objectives within the Asia-Pacific Region.[40] The maintenance of this relationship is a key component of the security strategy of the U.S. in the Asia-Pacific region, and is multi-faceted; it incorporates both fiscal and defense aid, among other options. For example, recently the Philippine Navy took possession of the decommissioned United States Coast Guard Cutter *Hamilton*, subsequently commissioning it as the BRP *Gregorio del Pilar* (PF-15), which will be the new flagship of the Philippine Navy.[41] Later this year, the Philippine Navy is expected to take possession of the United States Coast Guard Cutter *Dallas*, significantly increasing its surface naval presence.

---

[39]Department of Defense, *Sustaining U.S. Global Leadership: Priorities for 21st Century Defense* (Washington, DC: Government Printing Office, 2012), 2.

[40]The President of the United States, *2010 National Security Strategy*, 42.

[41]Embassy of the Philippines, "Philippine Navy Acquires Hamilton Cutter," May 5, 2011, http://www.philippineembassy-usa.org/news/1682/300/Philippine-Navy-Acquires-USCGC-Hamilton/d,phildet/ (accessed April 23, 2012).

Alliances are key to the attaining the strategic goals outlined in the *NSS*, with the concept of forging new alliances complementing the rebuilding of old alliances.[42] The theme of alliances and focusing on the Asia-Pacific region continues throughout most American strategic documents, including the newly published, *Priorities for 21st Century Defense*. In his promulgation letter to the Joint Force, Secretary of Defense Panetta asserts that "[the Joint Force] will have global presence emphasizing the Asia-Pacific."[43] In fact, the body of the document itself indicates that the security of the Asia-Pacific region represents a vital interest for the U.S. and is tied to the economic security of the nation. Indeed, even beyond that, the security of this region is directly tied to the security of the global community by providing a stabilizing influence. This linkage will also require a refocusing of military and defense strategies towards the region in order to secure the interest of the nation.[44]

---

[42]The President of the United States, *2010 National Security Strategy*, Letter of Promulgation.

[43]Department of Defense, *Sustaining U.S. Global Leadership: Priorities for 21st Century Defense* (Washington, DC: Government Printing Office, 2012), Letter of Promulgation.

[44]Ibid., 2.

CHAPTER 3

RESEARCH METHODOLOGY

Introduction

Chapter 3 describes the methodology employed to conduct a comparative analysis of the security strategies of the U.S. and the RP. The discussion will first briefly outline the research development concept, and then discuss the methodology. Ethical considerations and informed consent issues will also be addressed. Lastly, the chapter discusses the philosophical basis of the data analysis.

Research Development Concept

Recent literature, strategic documents, public statements (e.g., State Speeches), and other documents were reviewed in the effort to identify specific areas of shared concern within the strategies of these two nations. This review identified the shared strategic goals of the U.S. and the RP that pertain to the security strategy of the Southeast Asian region. The research also identified recommendations to highlight possible ways in which the U.S. and the RP may work in concert to advance these goals. Lastly, possible avenues for future research endeavors that may expound upon the theme and provide more in-depth venues for development were identified. Figure 2 is a conceptual model of the research process.

Figure 2.   Conceptual Model of Research Methodology

Source: Created by author.

Research Methodology

A qualitative approach to the project was selected due to the nature of the study as previously discussed in chapter 1. Further, qualitative field research increases the depth of the understanding that is attained during the process by requiring a continuous process of investigation and comparison, rather than merely collecting and analyzing data.[45] Qualitative research also provides more flexibility and leeway in pursuing emergent issues during the research process. As Anselm L. Strauss and Juliet M. Corbin state,

---

[45]Earl R. Babbie, *The Practice of Social Research*, 10th ed. (Belmont, CA: Wadsworth, 2004), 307.

"[q]ualitative research begins with a broad question and often no preidentified concepts," that allows the pursuit of lines of inquiry.[46]

Within the framework of explaining qualitative analysis, constant comparison provides a refined methodology for inquiry. Creswell notes that employment of a constant comparison grounds the research to the categories and theories that emerge from the data analysis by redirecting the researcher back to the basis of the study.[47] This constant comparative analysis forms a logical path that helps the researcher to develop conclusions that proceed from the analysis in a thoughtful manner to answer the posed research questions. The down side of qualitative research, however, is that qualitative research requires a careful bounding of the scope of the research. Without carefully bounding the research, furtive lines of inquiry may emerge that distract from the research and fail to contribute to answering the research questions.

Strict adherence to the study methodology that set the previously outlined limitations bounded the research. This is a normal procedure, when conducting research, for managing the scope of the research and retaining the focus of the research. Limitations and delimitations are set as the research commences in order to establish the boundaries of the research and preclude the development and pursuit of tangential research.

---

[46]Juliet Corbin and Anselm Strauss, *Basics of Qualitative Research: Techniques and Procedures for Developing Grounded Theory,* 3rd ed. (London: Sage Publications, 2008), 21.

[47]John W. Creswell, *Qualitative Inquiry and Research Design: Choosing Among Fiver Traditions* (Thousand Oaks, CA: Sage Publications, 1998), 57.

The research process only analyzed unclassified sources to answer the research questions. The research process consisted of an in-depth review of peer-reviewed literature, as well as a review of formal policy statements, doctrine state addresses, and speeches and other available sources of strategic insight from both the U.S. and the RP. The research process comparatively reviewed the strategies of the U.S. and the RP throughout, in an effort to identify parallels in the security strategies of the two nations. Examining the strategic security documents of the two respective nations facilitated the comparison of strategic ends. Additionally, a review and analysis of the constitutions of the two nations identified the grand strategies of the nations. By reflecting upon the grand strategies of the nations and their iteration within the national security strategies of the two countries, themes began to emerge and provide substance to answer the research questions.

Application of Lykke's model for identifying desired endstates and strategic goals for the two nations occurred after this examination and reflection upon the documents. The application of Lykke's model for determining strategic endstates aided in determining the ends, ways and means of security strategies and, subsequently, identified the complementary and concurrent themes between the strategic documents of the two nations. The ends, ways, and means of each nation, therefore, represent the points of congruence within the national security strategies of the nations under the application of this methodology. Further, by bounding the analysis within the Southeast Asian region, the analysis of these themes illuminated points of convergence between the security strategies of the U.S. and the RP.

Lykke provided a detailed explanation of his analysis model in his essay *Toward an Understanding of Military Strategy* that recounts and expounds upon the ends, ways, and means formula presented by Gen. Maxwell Taylor in 1981.[48] Within this essay, Lykke bounds the terminology of his formula using ends, ways, means, and risk, providing a necessary baseline for the understanding of the formula and a common reference point for all future discussions of strategy based on the model. In short, Lykke provides a detailed explanation and reasoned analysis of the model that Gen. Taylor advanced. This effort results in a workable and usable methodology for analyzing strategies.

Desired strategic goals constitute ends. One must understand the goal of any strategy in order to attain that strategic end just as one must know the destination for a voyage to be successful. In fact, without a stated end there would be no need to develop a strategy, much less to act upon that strategy. Ends require a plan of action, a concept of how to achieve the end. Lykke refers to these concepts as ways. Again, to return to the voyage metaphor, if one has a destination and a plan to get there, one must obtain transportation. Lykke refers to this component of strategy as the means; the resources one requires in order to arrive at the ends.

Lykke recognizes that there are circumstances when the components of ends, ways, and means contain a disparity. These disparities may arise, for example, due to a mismatch of desired ends and the ways or means to achieve them. This is not the only manner in which these disparities may arise, but provides an example of the issue. When

---

[48]Arthur F. Lykke, Jr., "Toward and Understanding of Military Strategy," in *Military Strategy: Theory and Application* (Carlisle Barracks, PA: Government Printing Office, 1989), 179-185.

this disparity exists and entails a possible detrimental outcome, a fourth component to Lykke's model emerges, which he identifies as strategic risk.[49] The formulation of any strategic options must contend with strategic risk.

Certainly, the best option is to mitigate the risk. However, in some extreme cases, a mitigation of risk may be impossible or impractical. In such circumstances, strategic planners must identify risk, which in itself may provide some mitigation by alerting the policy developer to the possible perils of their strategic designs. Much as a limited amount of fuel may affect the ability to complete a voyage, risk certainly bears on the ability to achieve strategic ends. Mitigation of this risk may include such efforts as speed regulations that serve to improve gas mileage and ensure that travelers reach their destination.

Though this description of Lykke's model tends to sterilize and systematize the formulation of strategic policy and make it appear to be a simple equation incorporating ends, ways, means, and risk, this is a red herring. Lykke's model attempts to marginalize the artistic requirement of strategic policy formulation, making such policy development seem easier and, possibly, more objective. However, while the artistic element of strategy formulation makes it a difficult and subjective process, it also distinguishes strategic art from other policy development methodologies. In short, just because strategic thought is difficult, it does not mean that planners should marginalize creative efforts.

Thus, the examination of the security strategies of the U.S. and the RP incorporated Lykke's model due to its recognition as a standard tool for strategic analysis. The incorporation of this model provided validity to the conclusions reached

---

[49]Ibid., 181.

36

pertaining to the points of congruence identified between the security strategies of the U.S. and the RP. The stated strategic security goals indicate the strategic endstates desired by each of the nations and Lykke's model identified the ways and means of the security strategies.

Informed Consent and Ethical Considerations

No inquiry, interviews, or communication with other persons which involved the need to determine informed consent or address ethical considerations were conducted during the course of the research project.

Data Analysis

Earl R. Babbie states "qualitative research methods involve a continuing interplay between data collection and theory."[50] The implication of Babbie's statement is that researchers must continually evaluate what the data means to the research, rather than merely evaluating the data during one specific phase of the research process. Analysis does not stop after data collection. Rather, positions must be open to reexamination and reevaluation throughout the process.

The analysis portion of the study, as well as the collection process itself, involved a consistent review of the data gleaned from the study, in order to ensure that focus was maintained on the desired outcomes of the study. This consistent and constant comparison and revision was conducted within the framework of a qualitative analysis and filtered through the lens of Lykke's ends, ways, and means model for strategy analysis in order to identify answers to the proposed research questions.

---

[50]Babbie, *The Practices of Social Research*, 370.

Chapter 3 presented an overview of the manner in which the data analysis was conducted. Chapter 4 presents the findings and the results of the data analysis.

CHAPTER 4

FINDINGS AND ANALYSIS

This chapter presents the findings of the study and begins with a recapitulation of

the results and analysis of the strategic policies of the U.S. and the RP strategic model

using Lykke, which has become a virtual standard for the effective analysis of

strategies.[51] An analysis of the *NSP* of the Philippines and the Security Strategy of the

U.S. follows this recap. Lastly, the chapter presents the answers to the research questions.

Analysis of the Strategic Policies of the U.S. and the Republic of the Philippines

The strategic policies of both nations were analyzed by overlaying Lykke's

strategic analysis model on the published security strategies of both nations. This

facilitated the identification of ends, ways, means in accordance with the Lykke model.

Further, potential risks involving the attainment of the strategic security goals of both

nations, as pertaining to terrorist threats in Southeast Asia were also identified and

examined. Additionally, selected formal policy statements were examined for

discontinuity between any published security policy and these statements.

In the broadest sense of Lykke's conceptualization of ends in the ends, ways and

means model, the *NSP* of the Philippines is strategically focused on the security of the

nation. Therefore, the overall end identified during the analysis of the *NSP* is a secure

environment for the nation. When framed within the realm of terrorism, the *NSP*'s

---

[51]Harry R. Yarger, "Toward a Theory of Strategy: Art Lykke and the Army War College Strategy Model," *U.S. Army War College Guide to National Strategy and Policy*, June 2006, 48.

identified end state remains a secure environment. The *NSP* specifically states that its goal is to "attain the state or condition wherein the national interests, the well-being of our people and institutions, and our sovereignty and territorial integrity are protected and enhanced."[52] The *NSP* envisions seven specific elements that contribute to national security strategy (see figure 3).

These seven elements that contribute the national security strategy are: peace and harmony, socio-political stability, territorial integrity, economic solidarity, moral-spiritual consensus, cultural cohesiveness, and ecological balance. These seven components are the ways in which the government of the Philippines envisions achieving the endstate of national security regarding terrorist threats to the nation. Intuitively, one must comprehend that the seven components are not mutually exclusive. Exclusively, these components minimally contribute to the national security objectives of the RP. The framework of the *NSP* explains these ways. Additionally, the *NSP* provides an initial vision for the means required to accomplish these ways.

Ends

As previously stated, the *NSP* of the Philippines communicates the desired endstate of the the RP is a secure nation. Specifically, the *NSP* elucidates that the national security policy of the nation should be focused upon the "[r]elevant constitutional provisions assert and define various aspects of the national security agenda . . . aimed at upholding and promoting peace, prosperity, freedom and democracy, consistent with the

---

[52]Republic of the Philippines, *2011-2016 National Security Policy: Securing the Gains of Democracy* (Manila: Bureau of Printing, 2011), 1.

40

values enshrined in the Consititution."[53] By aligning these mandates from the national documents, the *NSP* of the Philippines provides a continuity of effort and focus towards achieving the grand strategy of the nation.

Therefore, one may deduce from the overall security strategy of the *NSP*, that the ability of the nation to secure its environment from terrorist threats and activity is a key component of the security strategy of the nation. Terrorism is a national issue, and by passing HB04839 in 2006, the 13th Congress of the Republic of the Philippines demonstrated how serious it viewed the threat. This bill defined terrorism and established internal mechanisms for preventing and suppressing terrorist activity within the country.[54]

Ways

The *NSP* of the Philippines enumerates seven specific elements of national security that, when viewed through the eyes of the Lykke model, constitute the ways towards achieving the strategic ends of the *NSP*. These seven elements deserve a more detailed explanation that illuminates just how the *NSP* views them. Additionally, this section will provide an explanation of just how the efforts of the government incorporate these ways in their plans to attain a secure environment for the nation. The *NSP* does not list these elements of national security in any particular order, indicating that a coequality

---

[53]Ibid., 2.

[54]Philippines HB 04839 was re-crafted several times prior to being passed. It established parameters for defining and prosecuting acts of terror within the nation and may be viewed as the codification of the nation's resolve to combat terrorism within its territories.

of priority exists between the elements. They are presented here in the same order as within the *NSP*.

The first element listed by the *NSP* is the element of socio-political stability. From the perspective of the *NSP*, this elements encompasses a comprehensive sense of calm and equality amongst the population of the nation. This sense of calm permeates throughout the nation and fosters a mutual respect and tolerance for everyone, regardless of any traditional social discriminators (e.g., religion, race).[55] In short, socio-political stability includes the observation of internationally-accepted standards of human rights.

The *NSP* next mentions territorial integrity as a component of national security. The ability of the Philippines to control all of the land and sea area within its internationally-recognized borders is a key part of establishing and maintaining the legitimacy of the nation.[56] Although this may at first seem to be more pertinent to the international security of the nation, the geography of the Philippines transforms this component. Without effectively being capable of controlling its territory, the Philippine government sacrifices some level of legitimacy and possibly creates space and time for exploitation by terrorist elements. Futher, the ability to control territory contributes to the efforts of the other ways.

For example, the next element listed by the *NSP* is economic solidarity. Economic solidarity in such a vast location as the Philippines necessarily entails control of territory, as much of its internal commerce flows through mixed-modal transportation (e.g., sea to

---

[55]Republic of the Philippines, *2011-2016 National Security Policy: Securing the Gains of Democracy* (Manila: Bureau of Printing, 2011), 3.

[56]Ibid., 3.

land, or air to land). The RP must keep all lines of communication open and secured (i.e., territorial integrity). Further, the RP must conserve and protect its national resources in order to both feed the population and export agricultural products abroad.

The element of ecological balance complements, and is complemented by, economic solidarity. Natural resource conservation is a key element of many security strategies, due to the fact that many natural resources are limited and difficult or impossible to replace. The *NSP* of the Philippines sees ecological responsibility as a shared duty between all persons within the nation, at all levels of society.[57] Fostering the recognition of shared responsibilities within the societal structures of the nation contributes to the sense of cultural cohesiveness that the *NSP* views as a vital bonding between the people of the country.

Cultural cohesiveness reflects the shared characteristics of the people of the RP, whether they are linguistic, religious, artistic, or any other distinguishable trait that makes a Filipino a member of that society.[58] The *NSP* envisions the people of the Philippines as being willing to embrace their identity and that the government can capitalize on this in order to unify the nation and, therefore, contribute to internal security. Cultural divisiveness, conversely, erodes at the sense of nationalism and fosters discontent, distrust, and internal friction. These elements may then lead to national instability, terrorism, and a lack of national security. Cultural cohesiveness combats these destabilizing elements when coupled with the other elements of national security.

---

[57]Ibid., 4.

[58]Ibid.

Moral-spiritual consensus builds upon the sense of cultural cohesiveness to strengthen the commitment of the people of the RP in supporting their national government. Consolidating national unity is a key component in the *NSP* towards securing the nation and preventing terrorism.[59] As stated in the *NSP* "[t]his shared vision inspires and motivates the citizens to get involved and participate vigorously in the programs that promote the country's security and development goals and objectives."[60] In other words, cultivating this level of consensus promotes self-policing involvement by the citizens, who view themselves as vested stakeholders in the nation, rather than merely disinterested citizenry.

The last component of national security discussed within the *NSP* is the component of peace and harmony. The RP identifies itself as a democratic nation, "committed to world peace and the preservation of world order."[61] The specific mention of world order within the *NSP* of the Philippines represents a key linkage to the *NSS* of the United States, which identifies international order (i.e., world order) as one of the four key interests of the United States in attaining a secure environment.[62] Perhaps understandably, however, the RP narrows the focus of its influence on world order to the Association of Southeas Asian Nations (ASEAN), an organization that provides a starting

---

[59]Ibid.

[60]Ibid., 5.

[61]Ibid.

[62]As previously noted, the value of international order appears to be immense, due to the in-depth discussion of the issue within the U.S. *National Security Strategy of 2010.*

point for the nation to begin to attempt to influence world order and aid in the preservation of peace.[63]

These elements of national security, as delineated and explained within the *NSP* of the Philippines, provide the ways that the leadership of the RP views as necessary for the attainment of the strategic endstate. These ways represent a foundation, upon which, the nation may proceed to allocate resources and investments of guns or butter (i.e., the strategic means). Additionally, these ways represent the areas that may be identified as acceptable risk in the allocation of these resources. However, these ways do not represent mutually exclusive paths to national security. In short, the crafters of the *NSP* of the Phlippines acknowledge the synergistic benefit provided by the integration of all of these elements.

Means

Although a more detailed analysis of the strategic means that the RP has implemented (or intends to implement) is not within the scope of this project, broadly vieiwing the means envisioned by the President of the Philippines is possible. Within the *NSP*, the "Social Contract with the Filipino People" (SCFP), as outlined by President Benigno S. Aquino III, supports the strategic ways.[64] Although nonspecific in the allocatin of resources, the SCFP certainly communicates how the national president envisions accomplishing the strategic security objectives of the nation.

---

[63]Republic of the Philippines, *2011-2016 National Security Policy: Securing the Gains of Democracy* (Manila: Bureau of Printing, 2011), 5.

[64]Ibid.

The SCFP provides the mechanism to link the will of the Filipino people into the process of securing the nation. The Filipino people, and their collective will and desire for security, constitute the means to achieve this endstate. The SCFP is a comprehensive plan, envisioned and devised by President Aquino, that aligns the elements of national security into a complete and comoprehensive agenda.[65] This agenda integrates these elements into a complementary process, designed in order to maximize the economy of effort of the nation in achieving the endstate through the eomplyment of the strategic ways.

The RP has also engaged in a program of military recapitalization, as previously discussed. This recapitalization and modernization program builds upon the SCFP's linkage to the will of the people by providing a tangible and observable change to the status of the nation in its ability to provide for its security organically. Without these efforts, the mere desire of the people to attain a secure nation would simply not be enough.

---

[65]Ibid.

Figure 3.   Philippine *NSP* Perception of Elements of National Security

Source: Created by author.

Summary of the *NSP*

Figure 3 depicts the interrelated nature of the foundational structures of national

security, as elucidated by the *NSP*. None of these structures exists in a vacuum, but rather

they all impact each other in some way. Therefore, the *NSP* recognizes that any effort to eradicate terrorism, for example, may involve addressing issues of cultural cohesiveness and economic solidarity, among others.

NSP and Security Challenges

Externally, the *NSP* reiterates that the RP recognizes the U.S. as the sole remaining global superpower. Although not classified as a superpower by the *NSP*, it also recognizes China as a significant presence in the region, second only to the U.S. in stature. Notably, however, the *NSP* appears to consider China as a potential threat, stemming mainly from China's excursions and provocative movements in the South China Sea.[66] In short, the *NSP* appears to view the U.S., China, Japan, and ASEAN as the primary strategic partners in working to eradicate security threats, including terrorism, within the region. Strategic efforts to combat terrorism in the region must incorporate these partnerships. The *NSP* of the Philippines includes insurgencies and terrorism within the focus on the internal environment, yet must realize that potential external terrorist threats exist.

Interestingly, however, the *NSP* includes the MILF, which is the more militant wing of the Moro National Liberation Front (MNLF) within the issue of internal armed conflict. Contrasting this, the *NSP* categorizes the ASG as a terrorist threat in the region. The MILF has engaged in activities which may easily be viewed as being as violent as those of the ASG. Certainly, it is not unusual for governments, organizations, states, and others, to struggle with the exact way to best capture the issues confronting them. Perhaps the more discernable goals of the MILF have contributed to its credibility as an armed

---

[66]Ibid., 12-13.

insurgency rather than a mere terrorist organization, with loosely stated goals, such as the ASG.

Analysis of the National Security Strategy of the U.S.

This paper does not purport to engage in a comprehensive analysis of the *NSS* of the U.S. Rather, the analysis of the *NSS* will be conducted as it pertains to the defined regional focus of this paper. This is a necessary approach due to the fundamental divergence in the worldviews between the U.S. and the RP. The U.S. views itself as a global power, and the *NSS* of the United States reflects this self-perception and drives the U.S. towards a participatory tole in regional security trends. This tendency of great powers to attempt to become involved in regional security trends has been noted by scholars and researched.[67]

The great power strategic perspective of the U.S. differs from the regional strategic viewpoint of the RP, which views itself as a participant in global strategy rather than an influencer in global strategy. In other words, there is limited convergence of thought regarding security strategy at the macro level between the U. S. and the RP due to their relative positions in the international community. Convergence exists at this level based upon the underlying belief that building alliances and partnerships is a key component of achieving strategic security goals.

The *NSS* only specifically identifies the RP once within its text. This should not necessarily be viewed as a minimization of the importance of the RP to the overall security strategy of the U.S. in Southeast Asia. The *NSS* carefully avoids overly

---

[67]Pei-Chich Hao, "Great Powers' Strategy and Regional Integration: A New Regionalism Analytical Approach," *Issues and Studies* 45, no. 1 (March 2009): 163.

emphasizing any one nation in order to preserve the balance of influence and avoid eroding any regional influence.

Ends

The *NSS* focuses both on the security of the U.S. in particular, but views this goal as achievable through a secure international environment. The genesis of this perspective is understandable, as it arises from the position of the U.S. in the global community. Therefore, the *NSS* views security in the Southeast Asian region as attainable through exercising its influence in an attempt to change the environment, rather than allowing the environment to dictate how the U.S. operates.[68]

When juxtaposed with Lykke's strategic model, the identifiable ends emerge from the *NSS* as a secure environment in which the U.S. "champion[s] mutual interests among nations and peoples."[69] In other words, the U.S. is attempting to organize the common regional interests (e.g., freedom of navigation in the South China Sea) and then develop strategies to meet these interests. Focusing on Southeast Asia, the *NSS* includes the aforementioned endstate as the preferred outcome for the security of the region.

Ways

The previous discussion briefly touched on the disparity between the positions of the U.S. and the RP. When evaluating the ways of strategic success, the positional disparities become significant. Although the RP is certainly capable of exerting some influence within the Southeast Asian region, the U.S. is capable of exerting enormous

---

[68]United States of America, *2010 National Security Strategy*, 2010, 9.

[69]Ibid.

influence, albeit in some cases inadvertently, throughout the globe. Additionally, the U.S. consistently evaluates the entirety of the international community as a reflection of its operating environment, whereas the RP does not.

The U.S. conducts this process of continual evaluation of the operating environment by employing various entities and charging them with these evaluations. These entities include the regional combatant commanders (e.g., PACOM for the Pacific Area) as well sa the Department of State and other agency stakeholders in the region. The actions of these organizations and entities constitute a strategic way for the endstate to be reached, as these continual evaluations and engagement processes result in an opportunitiy to update and revise plans. Further, after these plans are revised, strategic means are assigned and reallocated as needed.

In sum, then, the U.S. possesses a more robust arsenal of strategic means to achieve their desired endstate of a secure environment in the Southeast Asian region. Projection of American interests into the region in the form of agency engagement, military assets (e.g., deployed Naval forces), economic assistance, and other resources, results in an opening for the U.S. to attempt to influence the environment in a manner that is favorable to the country. To extrapolate this concept and associate it with partnership initiatives, countries that partner with the U.S. reap benefits by proxy from the efforts tof the U.S.

Focusing within the Southeast Asian security dimension of strategy, the U.S. views the ways towards security through the continuance of partnership initiatives and attempting to assist in or influence regional policymaking.[70] Namely, the *NSS* focuses on emerging regional states, ASEAN, and other initiatives to create the stable and secure environment within Southeast Asia.

Means

The *NSS* does note specifically mention asset allocation, funding, or other resource apportionment towards the strategic ways. Instead the *NSS* accomplishes this process implicitly, by delegating the responsibilities to the Department of Defense. However, the *NSS* mentions policy issues that indicate the U.S. is committed to securing the Southeast Asian region. Engagement with nations, whether they be friendly, hostile, or neutral, is a way that translates into an implied set of means to achieve strategic goals (i.e., there can be no engegaement without resource allocation and expenditure).[71]

Again, it must be emphasized that the U.S. views security strategy from a position of influence, while the RP approaches the same issue from a position of being subject to influence. Therefore, the *NSS* emphasizes the importance of cooperation within the region, exerting influence, and awaiting determination of the intent of the regional actors as a way to achieve the strategic end. Therefore, the means allocated to these strategic ways consist of various efforts by the U.S. that are as diverse as special forces groups to train military forces and nation building initiatives sponsored by the Department of State.

---

[70]Ibid., 43.

[71]Ibid., 3.

Points of Convergence

The primary research questions focused on whether or not there are points of convergence between the security strategies of the U.S. and the RP, regarding the efforts to combat terrorism in the region. The research answered this question by examining and comparing the application of Lykke's strategic model of ends, ways, and means to the security strategies of both nations. Specifically, the research process involved applying Lykke's model to the issue of terrorism in the region of the RP.

After reviewing the *NSP*, the desired endstate that emerges from the perpective of the RP regarding terrorism is that of a secured internal environment. Although the *NSP* of the Philippines explores the issue of a secure external environment, the RP lacks the ability to realize this vision through any means other than by forming alliances and partnerships. In the vernacular of the Lykke model, the RP lacks the means to allocate to the ways to reach the ends. The Philippines recognizes that a secure external environment also plays an important role in reaching their desired endstate regarding terrorism. Specifically, the unstable external environment provides a potential destabilizing influence through the proliferation and availability of weapons to terrorist groups.[72]

When the *NSP* of the Philippines is examined through Lykke's lens, it becomes apparent that the RP has attempted to minimize its exposure to strategic risk pursuing its desired endstate by engaging in multiple partnerships. These alliances include the ASEAN multi-lateral alliance, its bi-lateral alliance with the U.S., as well as the recent efforts to engage in strategic engagement with the People's Republic of China. Ironically,

---

[72]Republic of the Philippines, *2011-2016 National Security Policy: Securing the Gains of Democracy* (Manila: Bureau of Printing, 2011), 14.

53

however, in some cases these alliances may result in provoking violent actors due to the perception that the RP government is aligned with antagonists to terror groups, such as the U.S.

The *NSP*'s intent aligns with the intent of the security strategy of the U.S. pertaining to the issue of terrorism. Notably, the RP shares the same perception as the U.S. that the environment has changed. Sovereign borders have become more porous and the result is a more integrated world that is harder to control and govern. Additionally, there is common verbiage within the *NSP*, including the identification that the centers of gravity have changed for many security factors. In short, the RP acknowledges that the international community has changed its focus from the West to the Asia-Pacific region.[73] This is not to say that the U.S. has lost its place of pre-eminence in the international community. Rather, simply that the exploitation of opportunities to increase resource, economic, and other gains has shifted from the West to the East. Additionally, the RP recognizes the fact that the mere presence of the U.S. in the region constitutes a stabilizing force and that the U.S. is, unless provoked, more than likely to engage in pursuing peaceful ways to solve problems.[74]

Most importantly, however, is the connection between the strategic views esposed by the U.S. and the RP concerning the importance of international order to the preservation of a secure environment. The presentation of this concept with virtually identical terminology, context, and sentiment lends to the presumption that perhaps the U.S. and the RP may have collaborated in the development of the *NSP* of the Philippines.

---

[73]Ibid., 7.

[74]Ibid., 12.

Almost certainly, it may be speculated that the various liaison officers of the nations communicated drafts of the policies between the countries.

This may appear at first blush to be a minor point of contention. Yet, upon further examination, it illuminates a more important issue. The recent announcement that the U.S. is shifting its attention towards the Asia-Pacific region[75] indicates that the RP may again gain importance to overall U.S. strategy in the region. Therefore, the alignment of U.S. and RP security strategies prior to this announcement indicates a possible concerted effort between the nations to develop a mutually-benficial and economical way forward. Extrapolating this further, by re-aligning with the RP, the U.S. tacitly aligned itself closer to ASEAN and, therefore, possibly reduced Chinese influence within the region.

At the very least, the similarity of strategic thought provides a clear communication to the regional protagonists and antagonists that the U.S. has at least one partner within the region. Further, the U.S. has indicated its willingness to work closely with this partner. Presumably, this willingness extends to the establishment of closer regional alignments with other ASEAN nations sue to the improving relationship with the RP.

---

[75]Department of Defense, *Sustaining U.S. Global Leadership: Priorities for 21st Century Defense* (Washington, DC: Government Printing Office, 2012), Letter of Promulgation.

CHAPTER 5

CONCLUSIONS AND RECOMMENDATIONS

Chapter 4 presented an overview of the analysis process and the application of the analysis to the research questions. From this analysis emerged several issues which may prove beneficial for future research or application to national security. This chapter will present these recommendations, as well as additional conclusions that emerged from the analysis of the issues.

Points of convergence exist between the national security strategies of the RP and the U. S. pertaining to the Southeast Asian region. The strategic ways envisioned by both nations, designed to achieve the strategic ends of a secure Southeast Asia, contain these convergence points. Both nations view partnerships and cooperative efforts as the most productive methods of advancing security initiatives within the region. Therefore, attempts to economize the efforts and achieve substantial progress towards the strategic endstate sould expand on these efforts. The U. S. should view the RP as a proxy actor, representing U. S. interests in the region to other regional states due to the apparent shared strategic goals of the two nations. Simply, the U. S. desires to communicate its influence within the region and the RP appears to be a sympathetic partner state that could do this.

Conversely, the RP should attempt to leverage its relationship with the U.S. in efforts to communicate its desire for a secure external environment throughout the region. Just as great power strategy exists, another complimentary strategy should also exist, which represents non-great powers. "Emergent state strategy" should develop ways of brokering influence from great powers towards attainment of strategic ends by forming symbiotic relationships with great powers. By aggressively pursuing such efforts, emergent states could relize more immediate results and transition to other agendas.

Further, emergent states' strategies should be codified in the lexicon of strategic thought by great powers such as the U.S., in order to ensure that they add this to consideration of strategic theory. Great powers ignore emergent states at the peril of the great power, as these emergent states are capable of generating a synergy with other emergent states. Such a synergy is observable within the ASEAN phenomenon, wherein a group of states have formed a partnership that continues to mature and has gained a prominent seat at the international table.

Recommendations

One of the implications of this study suggests that a more in-depth analysis of the strategic means that are being employed between the U.S. and the RP towards securing the Southeast Asian region should be undertaken. Although this project has uncovered some convergences between the security strategies of the two nations, true economic advantage would require a thorough review of just what means have been allocated towards these strategic ends in the region. Several agencies are positioned and capable of conducting such a review. The Institute for Southeast Asian Studies, PACOM, or the Asia-Pacific Center for Security Studies possess regional expertise as well as academic capital and could easily undertake such a project in order to provide meaningful insight into the issue.

Additionally, the U.S. should invest in efforts to advance and preserve President Aquino's SCFP as a way to buttress the human capital of the RP and channel the will of the people to advance the security agenda of the nation. Similar initiatives could be suggested and supported throughout the region by U.S. agencies in order to capitalize on the presumed inherent desire of most people(s) to live in a secure and peaceful environment.

Future Research

Foremost, the U.S. and the RP must address the status of the 1951 MDT. This issue emerged as a consistent and persistent theme during the research process. Under Article VIII of the MDT, the treaty does not expire—it is open-ended, much like the Taiwan Relations Act.[76] Additionally the current *NSP* of the Philippines alludes to the perception by the RP that the treaty plays a central role in strategic security planning for the nation.[77]

The question is not merely whether or not the MDT remains in effect. Rather, the more important question is just how committed the U.S. is to the MDT. Buss noted that the MDT stipulations include "armed attack on the metropolitan territory of either of the parties."[78] The question remains open as to whether or not armed attack includes terrorist or insurgent activity under the MDT. Further, while each respective nation's constitutional machinations would certainly be incorporated into any response under the MDT, the question emerges as to whether or not nations should have treaties in effect that are not vigorously adhered to. Such alliances influence the environment and have impact

---

[76]Steven M. Goldstein and Randall Schriver, "An Uncertain Relationship: The United States, Taiwan and the Taiwan Relations Act," *China Quarterly* 165 (March 2001): 172.

[77]Republic of the Philippines, *2011-2016 National Security Policy: Securing the Gains of Democracy* (Manila: Bureau of Printing, 2011), 12.

[78]Buss, *The United States and the Philippines: Background for Policy*, 113.

on the actions that third parties take in response to changes in the environment, thus potentially either stabilizing or destabilizing the environment.

This recommendation is germaine to the primary research question due to the vibrant nature of terrorist activity since the inception of the treaty in 1951. The primary concern at the time of the treaty's creation was the communist threat spreading throughout Southeast Asia, not the possibility of continued, persistent terrorist attacks upon either nation. Arguably, although state actors remain in the Southeast Asian region who harbor designs on obtaining natural resources in the area and expanding territorial claims, the main threats to the region exist in the form of terrorism or non-state actors.

An additional venue for future research exists in the exploration of a similar comparative analysis of the strategic interests of the RP and other major actors in the region. Such analyses may provide insight into the concerns of other regional actors as well as insight into the emerging priorities for regional stability and security. While the RP remains far from being categorized as a regional super power, the nation certainly provides a key strategic ally and conduit for the U.S. in gaining credibility and access in the region.

The Grierson Competition at the U.S. Army Command and General Staff College, in which students compete for recognition as the Distinguished Master Strategist from their graduating class, provides a means to further address issues of this line of inquiry.[79] This year the College has focused on Southeast Asian security study issues. Embracing the recently released 2012 Defense Strategy's recognition of the area as an area of

---

[79]*Leavenworth Lamp*, http://www.ftleavenworthlamp.com/news/x1569718235/Awards-recognize-top-students-of-class-2011-02 (accessed May 7, 2012).

increasing importance, the directors of the competition have directed competitors to research, discuss, and support strategies for developing and sustaining international order in the region. Albeit an informal research project, it illustrates the simple fact that the Southeast Asian focus has filtered even to the introductory level education of military strategists and should spur additional, higher-level research projects.

GLOSSARY

Ends. Objectives towards which one strives.[80]

Grand Strategy. A broad delineation of national interests, goals, and ambitions set forth as a roadmap for national direction.[81]

Means. Instruments by which some end can be achieved.[82]

Securitization. A model of forming an understanding of non-material concepts based on social sciences. Additionally, once a concept becomes recognized by societies or cultures, the re-evaluation of these concepts eventually may convince audiences that these concepts are now security issues.[83]

Ways. Course of action.[84]

---

[80] Arthur F. Lykke, Jr., "Toward and Understanding of Military Strategy," in *Military Strategy: Theory and Application* (Carlisle Barracks, PA: Government Printing Office, 1989), 179.

[81] Daniel Drezner, "Does Obama Have a Grand Strategy?" *Foreign Affairs* 90, no. 4 (July/August 2011): 58.

[82] Arthur F. Lykke, Jr., "Toward and Understanding of Military Strategy," in *Military Strategy: Theory and Application* (Carlisle Barracks, PA: Government Printing Office, 1989), 179.

[83] Tom O'Connor, "The Concept of Securitization," MegaLinks in Criminal Justice, http://www.drtomoconnor.com/2010/2010lect01a.htm (accessed November 1, 2011; Shofwan A. Choiruzzed, GlobalWar on Terror, Securitization, and Human (In)Security: Indonesia's Case http://ritsumei.academia.edu/ShofwanAlbannaChoiruzzad/ Papers/434199/Global_War_on_Terror_Securitization_and_Human_In_Security_Indones ias_Case (accessed September 16, 2011).

[84] Arthur F. Lykke, Jr., "Toward and Understanding of Military Strategy," in *Military Strategy: Theory and Application* (Carlisle Barracks, PA: Government Printing Office, 1989), 179.

REFERENCE LIST

Books

Babbie, Earl. *The Practice of Social Research.* 10th ed. Belmont, CA: Wadsworth, 2004.

Buss, Claude A. *The United States and the Philippines: Background for Policy.* Washington, DC: American Enterprise Institute for Public Policy Research, 1977.

Corbin, Juliet, and Anselm Strauss. *Basics of Qualitative Research: Techniques and Procedures for Developing Grounded Theory.* 3rd ed. London: Sage Publications, 2008.

Lykke, Arthur F., Jr. "Toward and Understanding of Military Strategy." In *Military Strategy: Theory and Application.* Carlisle Barracks, PA:. Government Printing Office, 1989.

Weatherbee, Donald E. *International Relations in Southeast Asia: The Struggle for Autonomy.* New York: Rowman and Littlefield, 2005.

Periodicals/Journals

Acharya, Amitav. "A Regional Security Community in Southeast Asia?" *Strategic Studies and Security* 18, no. 3 (1995): 175-200.

Baker, Nicola, and Leonard C. Sebastian. "The Problem with Parachuting: Strategic Studies and Security in the Asia/Pacific Region." *Strategic Studies and Security* 18, no. 3 (1995): 15-31.

Corning, Gregory P. "The Philippine Bases in U.S. Pacific Strategy." *Pacific Affairs* 63, no. 1 (Spring 1990): 6-23.

Cruz De Castro, Renato. "Engaging Both the Eagle and the Dragon: The Philippines' Precarious and Futile Attempt in Equi-balancing." *Pacific Focus* 25, no. 3 (December 2010): 356-375.

Drezner, Daniel W. "Does Obama Have a Grand Strategy?" *Foreign Affairs* 90, no. 4 (July-August 2011): 57-68.

Hao, Pei-Chih. "Great Powers' Strategyand Regional Integration: A new Regionalism Analytical Approach." *Issues and Studies* 45, no. 1 (March 2009): 163-202.

Ryan, Alan. "The Strong Lead-Nation Model in an ad hoc Coalition of the Willing: Operation Stabilise in East Timor." *International Peacekeeping* 9, no. 1 (Spring 2002): 23-34.

Research/Keynote/Seminar/Symposium/Information Papers

Choiruzzed, Shofwan A. Global War on Terror, Securitization,a dn Human (In)Security: Indonesia's Case. http://ritsumei.academia.edu/ShofwanAlbannaChoiruzzad/ Papers/434199/Global_War_on_Terror_Securitization_and_Human_In_Security_ Indonesias_Case (accessed September 16, 2011).

O'Connor, T. "The Concept of Securitization." *MegaLinks in Criminal Justice*, March 9, 2011. http://www.drtomoconnor.com/2010/2010lect01a.htm (accessed November 1, 2011).

Internet Sources

Findlaw. "Maintenance of National Security and the First Amendment." http://caselaw.lp. findlaw.com/data/constitution/amendment01/13.html (accessed March 11, 2012).

Government Documents

Chairman, Joint Chiefs of Staff. Joint Publication (JP) 1, *Dictionary of Military and Associated Terms*. Washington, DC: Government Printing Office, 1985.

Department of Defense. *Sustaining U.S. Global Leadership: Priorities for 21st Century Defense*. Washington, DC: Government Printing Office, 2012.

President of the Philippines. "Memorandum Order No. 6: Directing the Formulation of the National Security Policy and National Security Strategy for 2010-2016." http://www.gov.ph/2010/10/21/memorandum-order-no-6/ (accessed October 22, 2011).

Republic of the Philippines. *2011-2016 National Security Policy: Securing the Gains of Democracy*. Manila, Philippines: Bureau of Printing, 2011.